A Cut in the Rates

A play

Alan Ayckbourn

Samuel French - London
New York - Toronto - Hollywood

ISBN 0 573 12084 6

Please see page iv for further copyright information

CHARACTERS

Miss Pickhart
Woman/Rosalinda
Ratchet

A Cut in the Rates

First transmitted on BBC TV Schools in their "English File" series on 21st January, 1984 with the following cast of characters:

Miss Pickhart	Lavinia Bertram
Woman/Rosalinda	Liza Sadovy
Ratchet	Michael Cashman

The action takes place in a street, a study and a cellar

Time — the present

A Cut in the Rates

The outside of a Victorian terrace house. The front door. An upstairs window is open . It is mid-morning

After a moment, Miss Pickhart comes trotting down the street. She stops at the house and, having taken a rather nervous deep breath, raps on the door with the knocker. She waits, clutching her briefcase. She knocks again

Miss Pickhart *(calling)* Hallo, hallo. *(She knocks some more)*

A woman leans out of the window upstairs

Woman You'll find no-one there, love.
Miss Pickhart Sorry, beg your pardon?
Woman It's all shut up. You'll find no-one.
Miss Pickhart Really? I was under the impression——
Woman Not for seven years. Neither of them.
Miss Pickhart I'm on official business from the Town Hall. Will you let me in, please?
Woman It's nothing to do with me. I'm upstairs. *(She starts to go)*
Miss Pickhart I say, just a moment. I say. I'm from the Town Hall.
Woman Stuff the Town Hall. *(She withdraws her head from the window)*
Miss Pickhart Really. *(She hesitates and starts to go. Then, with fresh resolution)* No. I'm not being fobbed off with that. *(She knocks on the door again)* Come on. If you don't open up, I shall be back with someone to open it for me. Come along. Oh——

The door suddenly swings open as she starts to knock afresh

She sticks her nose round the door and enters cautiously

The interior is rather bleak. She is in a hallway leading to a study with a desk, a desk chair, a filing cabinet and a rocking chair. It all seems curiously deserted

Anyone here? Soneone's here. I know you're here, somebody. Come along, who's here?

Ratchet steps out of the shadows. He is a man of indeterminate age, pale and gaunt, and dressed rather incongruously in white tie and tails

(*Starting*) Ah.

Ratchet Good-day.

Miss Pickhart Good ... morning. Are you ... are you Mr Ratchet? Mr T.L. Ratchet?

Ratchet Thomas Ratchet.

Miss Pickhart Good. It's you I've come to see. I knew you were in. You're the owner of this house?

Ratchet I was. I was indeed.

Miss Pickhart Was?

Ratchet No longer, alas. I moved on.

Miss Pickhart Well, that's not according to our information. I'm from the Rating Office and you are clearly listed in our records as being the owner.

Ratchet Indeed. How strange.

Miss Pickhart And I'm afraid it's you I'm calling upon concerning the little matter of unpaid rates.

Ratchet Terrible, how terrible.

Miss Pickhart It is getting very serious. As you well know. You must do. We've written to you on (*consulting her files*) seven occasions. January twelfth, January twenty eighth, February tenth ...

Ratchet I'm sorry. I'm afraid I've been rather out of touch.

Miss Pickhart You've been away?

Ratchet In a sense.

Miss Pickhart It says here you're an entertainer. Is that so?

Ratchet Some years ago. Not any more.

Miss Pickhart You're retired?

Ratchet Permanently.

Miss Pickhart I see. You seem rather young for ——

Ratchet It was enforced.

Miss Pickhart Oh dear. Were you made redundant?

Ratchet Totally. Please sit down.

Miss Pickhart Thank you. (*She sits*) You know, there are schemes you can ...

Ratchet You look a little tired.

Miss Pickhart Well, yes, a little. I'm not used to ... actually, it's my first day back at work.

Ratchet Holidays?

Miss Pickhart No, no. Illness. I had a — I was a little ill.

Ratchet Seriously?

Miss Pickhart No. Yes. Quite. It was — well, it was a little nervous trouble. My — my fiancé he was ... he was ...

Ratchet You have my every sympathy. I grieve your loss.

Miss Pickhart With another woman.

Ratchet Oh, I see.

Miss Pickhart She was— she was— she just ... she ... she just ... I'm over it now. The little ... So. Enough of me. We did discover, by the by, and I'm sure you're aware of this too, that the Gas and Electricity Boards are also pressing you quite heavily for payment.

Ratchet (*nostalgically*) Ah, the dear old Gas Board.

Miss Pickhart If you'll pardon my asking, do you live alone?

Ratchet Alone?

Miss Pickhart I don't mean to pry.

Ratchet I'm never alone.

Miss Pickhart Ah.

Ratchet I wish to God I was.

Miss Pickhart I'm merely trying to establish, you see, whether you're ...

Ratchet My wife died.

Miss Pickhart I am sorry.

Ratchet Seven years ago.

Miss Pickhart Was she ... she must have been very young.

Ratchet Twenty-five.

Miss Pickhart Ah.
Ratchet Beautiful.
Miss Pickhart Yes.
Ratchet Eyes that promised everything.
Miss Pickhart Lovely.
Ratchet To anyone.
Miss Pickhart Ah.
Ratchet And everyone.

Pause

Miss Pickhart With regard to the Rates, it has been drawn to our notice
that despite the fact that this house is listed as an S.D.U. — a single
domicillary unit, it is presently utilized as an M.D.U. — a multiple
domicillary unit, thus requiring that the property undergoes a totally
fresh rating re-appraisal. (*She pauses*) How did she die?
Ratchet Hmm?
Miss Pickhart Your wife.
Ratchet She met with an accident. At work.
Miss Pickhart An industrial accident?
Ratchet Not exactly.

Pause

Miss Pickhart I shall have to inspect the house, you know. Make a
report. I mean, I know you've made conversions. I spoke to the woman
upstairs.
Ratchet My pleasure. Follow me.
Miss Pickhart Thank you.

*They leave the study. Ratchet leads her to a flight of dingy stairs. They
start to descend*

Where are we going? Are we going to the cellar?
Ratchet Mind your head.
Miss Pickhart It's very dark, isn't it?

*They enter the cellar. It is dimly lit by a naked light bulb. There are
several odd, curious boxes and props strewn about*

Oh, yes. The cellar. Well, there's nothing wrong here. *(She sniffs)*
Except I think you've got some damp. You ought to get that seen to.
(Discovering the props) Heavens, what's all this? Is this part of your...
when you were an entertainer? All your tricks.

Ratchet Tricks?

Miss Pickhart Were you a magician?

Ratchet Magician?

Miss Pickhart I adore magicians. That man on television's wonderful.
(She comes across a saw-the-woman-in-half cabinet) I mean, things
like this are just ...

Ratchet No!

Miss Pickhart Isn't this one of those...

Ratchet *(shouting)* Don't touch that box!

Silence

Miss Pickhart I'm sorry.

Ratchet I'm sorry.

Miss Pickhart I do see. You don't want your tricks meddled around
with.

Ratchet I was an illusionist, madam. Not a magician.

Miss Pickhart No.

Ratchet Not a conjuror.

Miss Pickhart No.

Ratchet Not a prestidigitator.

Miss Pickhart No.

Ratchet An illusionist. And that box there contains the secret of the
most famous, the most well-loved illusion of all time. Millions of
people know how it's done or think they do and yet millions still love
to watch it. The illusion of the woman sawn in half.

Miss Pickhart Oh, yes. Splendid.

Ratchet Always a woman. It was on the night of the Junior Rotarians'
Christmas Party seven years ago. Rosalinda and I, we tried to — it all
went wrong. Horribly wrong. We tried to improve the illusion, you

see. Add a little spice to the familiar dish. We rehearsed it here. She knew it was dangerous. And then our first performance. I shouldn't have let her. So hot in that hotel lounge. People laughing. All that cigar smoke. She started screaming. I thought at first she was pretending. Then the whole room was screaming. So much blood. She was dead when she arrived at the hospital.

Miss Pickhart You mean your——

Ratchet Yes.

Miss Pickhart In half?

Ratchet It was a terrible mistake. I was acquitted. The coroner said — he said it was a tragic case of a misguided search for artistic perfection.

Miss Pickhart Oh, dear God. I don't know how you can come down here.

Ratchet I rarely do.

Miss Pickhart Dreadful for the Rotarians, too.

Ratchet (*suddenly*) Excuse me. I think I hear a bell. Excuse me a moment, please.

He leaves rapidly, disappearing into the gloom

Miss Pickhart Yes, right. I'll come with you, Mr ... (*Finding she is alone*) Hallo? Don't leave me down here. Honestly. It's terribly dark. (*To herself*) All right, Monica, pull yourself together. I say, I say.

Rosalinda steps unexpectedly from the shadows. She is dressed as a conjuror's assistant, but wears at present a short dressing gown to cover this

(*Seeing Rosalinda*) Oh, dear heavens. Who are you?

Rosalinda (*softly*) Please, don't be afraid.

Miss Pickhart I'm sorry, I have to go upstairs now. I have to look over the rest of the ——

Rosalinda Please. Please help me.

Miss Pickhart What?

Rosalinda Please. I heard what my husband was saying to you.

Miss Pickhart Your husband?

Rosalinda About the— about the accident.

Miss Pickhart Accident?

Rosalinda The so-called accident.

Miss Pickhart But he— he said you were dead. You're his wife? He told me just now——

Rosalinda I heard him.

Miss Pickhart Well, you're not. Are you? Dead.

Rosalinda Would that I were.

Miss Pickhart Pardon?

Rosalinda Do you understand what I mean by undead?

Miss Pickhart Undead?

Rosalinda He knew. It was no accident. He knew when he started sawing through the box that Christmas Eve in the *King's Head* lounge. The singing and the streamers and the paper hats and then the pain. Oh, the pain. He knew. He knew what he was doing. You must help me. Please. Help me to rest.

Miss Pickhart Listen. I've had a great deal of nervous trouble recently. I'm sorry, I can't——

Rosalinda Please. Please.

Miss Pickhart What do you want? I mean, I work for the Town Hall. I'm not ... what do you want?

Rosalinda (*standing by the cabinet*) You must ... You must take my place here for a moment. I'm unable to move far, you see. Or else the pain ... Take my place for a moment and you release me.

Miss Pickhart What about me?

Rosalinda You'll be safe. There's no danger.

Miss Pickhart What? Lie in that?

Rosalinda Just for a second.

Miss Pickhart Certainly not.

Rosalinda Then you condemn me to an eternity of this.

Rosalinda takes off her dressing-gown. She is in a two piece showgirl's outfit. Around her middle is a bloodstained bandage

Miss Pickhart Oh, dear heavens.

Rosalinda For a moment. Just for a moment. Please.

Miss Pickhart What do you want me to do then? I'm not ... I've never done this ...

Rosalinda (*opening up the cabinet*) It's simple. It's so simple. Look. You step in here ——

Miss Pickhart Yes. Well, help me, help me ——

Rosalinda (*doing so*) Yes.

Miss Pickhart (*climbing in*) Thank you.

Rosalinda (*showing her*) Now, you lie here with your feet through here —that's it—and then your head goes here. (*She traps Miss Pickhart's head*)

Miss Pickhart Ah. This is terribly claustrophobic.

Rosalinda (*excitedly*) That's it. That's it. That's how it has to be, you see. So you're completely helpless. Like I was on that night when he — (*Singing*) The Holly and the Ivy ... (*Speaking*) What was wrong with having a little fun? A little Christmas fun. Eh? Eh?

Miss Pickhart (*nervously*) Nothing. No. No harm. Why not?

Rosalinda Only the little man got jealous. He couldn't himself and he wasn't having others— so he— he ... (*She breaks off*) Sssh. He's coming back.

Miss Pickhart Well, don't leave me here like this.

Rosalinda (*drawing back into the shadows*) Sssh. (*Whispering*) Watch his face. Just watch his face.

Miss Pickhart This really isn't a frightfully good idea, is it?

Ratchet enters

Ratchet I'm sorry. I had to talk to ... (*He sees Miss Pickhart. Stunned*) Rosalinda? Rosalinda?

Miss Pickhart No, no. I'm afraid it's me. Monica Pickhart from the Town Hall.

Ratchet Rosalinda? So you think you can cheat me again, do you? You want to cheat me again?

Miss Pickhart No, now, please. I'm from the rating office, I ——

Ratchet (*unearthing a murderous looking large-toothed saw*) Here we go again ...

Miss Pickhart Oh, please no.

Ratchet I'll have to teach you another lesson. (*Singing*) The Holly and the Ivy ...

Miss Pickhart Help, somebody, please.

Ratchet Why aren't you singing, Rosalinda?

Miss Pickhart No, I'd rather not.

Ratchet (*singing*) When they are both full grown ... (*Speaking*) Come on, sing up. It's Christmas, you bitch. (*Singing*) The Holly and the Ivy ...

Miss Pickhart (*singing*) The Holly and the Ivy — (*screaming*) help!

Ratchet That's better. (*He starts to saw. Singing*) When they are both full grown——

Miss Pickhart (*singing with Ratchet*) When they are both full — (*screaming*) help!

Ratchet (*continuing his grim task, singing*) God rest ye merry gentlemen——

Rosalinda steps back into view

Rosalinda Tommy.

Ratchet (*stopping*) What?

Rosalnda I'm here, Tommy. I'm over here.

Ratchet Rosalinda?

Rosalinda I've come for you now, Tommy.

Ratchet (*dropping to his knees*) Aaarrrgghh!! (*He chokes and appears to have some sort of seizure*)

Rosalinda (*moving swiftly to release Miss Pickhart*) Quickly. Quickly. Are you all right?

Miss Pickhart (*singing*) I saw three ships come sailing by——

Rosalinda (*releasing Miss Pickhart*) There.

Miss Pickhart Sailing by——

Rosalinda Quickly.

Miss Pickhart Sailing by ——

Rosalinda Run. Run before he recovers. He'll be like this for a minute or so. No more.

Miss Pickhart (*clambering out of the cabinet*) Yes, yes. Right. (*Singing*) Ding dong merrily on high ——

Rosalinda Run. Run.

Miss Pickhart (*running*) Yes. Yes.

Ratchet Rosalinda ...

Rosalinda Quick. Before he kills you like he killed me.

Miss Pickhart (*hurrying up the cellar steps, singing to herself*) Good
  King Wenceslas looked out ... (*Speaking*) Where am I? Where's the
  front door? (*Singing*) On the feast of Stephen ——
Ratchet (*getting to his feet and following her*) Rosalinda. (*He is still
  carrying the saw*)

Miss Pickhart is now in the study and searching for the front door

Miss Pickhart (*singing*) We three Kings of Orient are ... I shouldn't
  be doing this. I've has a lot of nervous trouble.
Ratchet Rosalinda? I know you're hiding, Rosalinda?
Miss Pickhart Oh, no. (*She dives under the desk*)

Ratchet passes her, flexing his saw

Ratchet (*softly as he passes*) Rosalinda. Come to me, Rosalinda.
Miss Pickhart (*softly to herself, as he passes*) Star of wonder, star of
  light ... star of royal beauty bright ——

Ratchet goes out another door

*Miss Pickhart darts for the front door. She open and shuts it behind her
and stands in the open air breathing heavily*

  My files. I left my briefcase. All my papers. Oh ...

The Woman sticks her head out of the upstairs window

Woman (*shouting down*) I told you.
Miss Pickhart What?
Woman I told you, didn't I? I said there'd be nobody in.
Miss Pickhart Yes.
Woman Both passed on, you see. Seven years ago.
Miss Pickhart What?
Woman Died.
Miss Pickhart Yes. Good-morning.
Woman (*calling after her*) Crime of passion it was.

Miss Pickhart Really.
Woman He slit her open from here to here. (*She gestures*)
Miss Pickhart Goodbye.

Miss Pickhart goes

Woman (*to herself*) It's a lovely morning.

Ratchet comes out of the front door. He looks after Miss Pickhart and then, glancing up, sees the woman sunning herself in the window

Ratchet Hey.
Woman Mm?
Ratchet What are you doing?
Woman Getting some air.
Ratchet Well, don't hang around up there. Get back downstairs. We've got that fellow from the Gas Board at twelve-thirty.
Woman Oh, heck. Right. Why we can't pay our bills same as everybody else ...? (*She withdraws her head from the window, muttering*)
Ratchet (*contentedly sunning himself in the doorway*) No chance. Life's too short, love. Life's too short.

The Lights fade to Black-out

FURNITURE AND PROPERTY LIST

Only essential furniture and properties mentioned in the text are listed here. Further dressing may be added at the director's discretion

On stage: Desk
Desk chair
Filing cabinet
Rocking chair
Curious boxes
Large-toothed saw
Props
Saw-the-woman-in-half cabinet

Off stage: Briefcase containing files (**Miss Pickhart**)

Personal: **Rosalinda:** Bloodstained bandage

LIGHTING PLOT

Property fittings required: single bulb in cellar area
1 exterior, 2 interior settings

To open: General exterior lighting

Cue 1	**Miss Pickhart** enters cautiously *Cross-fade to dim lighting*	(Page 2)
Cue 2	**Miss Pickhart** shuts the front door *Cross-fade to exterior lighting*	(Page 10)
Cue 3	**Ratchet:** "Life's too short." *Fade to black-out*	(Page 11)

9 780573 120848